Introduction

WHEN IN 1864 Henry Armstead sculpted portraits of 'the most eminent artists of all ages of the world' around the base of the Albert Memorial, he included just one Dutchman, Rembrandt. The name of Rembrandt had become synonymous with Dutch seventeenth-century painting during the nineteenth century and has continued to be in this century. In reaction to this, there have been in recent years conscientious attempts to place Rembrandt within the context of painting in seventeenth-century Holland in order to show that he shared much with his less celebrated contemporaries. Both views by exaggeration can miss the truth. It *is* quite wrong that Rembrandt has come to stand for Dutch painting, but for the reason that he is a quite exceptional figure. His work is in no sense representative of Dutch painting as a whole. He was undoubtedly influenced by various of his contemporaries in Holland but he cannot be placed amidst them with any ease. It is not that he always towered above them, as has often been said, for he painted a number of indifferent pictures, particularly in his early years. Rather, he stood apart, and this separateness was recognized in his own century and made him a controversial figure.

Rembrandt's career defeats almost any generalization which can be made about Dutch seventeenth-century painting. Specialization, for example, is a characteristic of the time and place. Frans Hals painted portraits, Jacob van Ruisdael painted and etched landscapes, Johannes Vermeer (almost exclusively) painted *genre* scenes, Willem van de Velde marine paintings, Pieter Saenredam and Jan van der Heyden architectural views, and Pieter Claesz. still-life. Such specialization seems to have been encouraged by the mechanics of the Dutch art market, the first in the modern sense, which was dominated by the now familiar apparatus of dealers and auctions. Painters established a reputation for a particular kind of picture and the market maintained the demand and discouraged experimentation. Rembrandt, by contrast, although he thought of himself in the first place as a 'history' painter (that is, a painter of religious, mythological and historical scenes), painted a large number of portraits, some landscapes and even some *genre* scenes. He was also a prodigious etcher and draughtsman and had the largest number of pupils at any studio in Amsterdam. Among the major Dutch painters only Jan Steen approaches Rembrandt in the range of his art, and he painted few portraits, fewer landscapes and did not etch.

A second generalization contradicted by Rembrandt's career is that there was little religious painting in Holland during the century. Certainly it is true that the Calvinist influence in the Dutch Republic caused a virtual end to the display of religious paintings in churches, and the paintings of altarpieces, the staple of many artists' workshops in Flanders, almost ceased in Holland. In his early years Rembrandt painted a number of large religious pictures in a Baroque manner but he soon realized that these had few potential purchasers. It was his achievement to create a new type of small-scale religious painting which found an honoured place on the walls of the devout.

Rembrandt van Rijn was born in 1606 in Leiden. He was the son of a miller, Harmen Gerritsz. His father's occupation may suggest that his parents were poor, but his mother's will reveals that the family lived in comfortable circumstances. It was a deeply religious household and it was appropriate that Rembrandt in his early years used his parents as models for Biblical figures in his paintings. After seven years at the Latin school in Leiden, Rembrandt was enrolled in 1620 at the town's university. He was not there for long, entering instead the studio of a local painter, Jacob Isaacz. van Swanenburgh, who specialized in architectural views and scenes of Hell. After three years in Swanenburgh's provincial studio, Rembrandt went to Amsterdam to work with Pieter Lastman. Lastman was an artist of a quite different calibre from the obscure Swanenburgh. He had lived and worked in Italy for several years, and on his return to Amsterdam had established himself as a major figure in the city's artistic life. The principal influences on his style were Caravaggio (for his striking light effects) and Adam Elsheimer (for his precise and detailed technique). Lastman painted small pictures, almost invariably on panel, of religious, mythological or classical subjects. They display his unique combination of dramatic Baroque effects, a muscular, contorted figure style and a delight in the intricacy and rich surfaces of ornament and naturalistic detail. Whereas Rembrandt's early work — his first dated picture is from 1625 — shows no influence from Swanenburgh whatsoever, it does show a considerable dependence on Lastman.

Rembrandt spent only six months with Lastman, in 1624. He then returned to Leiden to set up his own studio which he shared with another pupil of Lastman, Jan Lievens. The two young artists worked together very closely (and may even have collaborated) until Rembrandt's departure for Amsterdam in 1631. It was during this time in Leiden that Rembrandt and Lievens were spotted as promising newcomers by Constantijn Huygens, secretary of the Prince of Orange, Frederik Henry. In his autobiography Huygens wrote that the miller's son Rembrandt and the embroiderer's son Lievens were equal to the most famous painters of the day and would soon surpass them. He predicted a great future for Rembrandt as a painter of historical compositions, adding that although Lievens was an excellent painter he would not easily attain Rembrandt's skill: 'For in historical works, as we commonly term them, no artist however great and admirable will easily equal the vivid invention of Rembrandt.'

It is hardly surprising that, having expressed this opinion, Huygens arranged an important commission for Rembrandt. During the 1630s Rembrandt painted the five pictures of the Passion series (*plate 6*) for Frederik Henry. The popular image of Rembrandt is of an artist who was independent, even truculent, remaining true to his own vision despite adversity. This may contain an element of truth when applied to his later years, but it is not at all borne out by his dealings with Huygens and the Prince. In his letters to Huygens he is ready to play the courtier, and when painting for Frederik Henry he was very conscious of the example of Rubens, the artist whom Huygens admired above all others. *The Descent from the Cross* (*plate 6*) directly depends in its composition on Rubens' great altarpiece in the Cathedral at Antwerp, and *The Blinding of Samson* (*plate 7*), which Rembrandt painted for Huygens himself, is an extraordinarily violent and dramatic *tour-de-force* in Rubens' Baroque manner.

Rembrandt's early success with the court circle at The Hague was as a history painter, the highest category of painting according to the most influential Dutch theorist of the first half of the seventeenth century, Carel van Mander. However, he also painted portraits of Huygens' brother, Maurits, and of Frederik Henry's wife, Amalia van Solms, both in 1632, and it was as a portrait painter that Rembrandt had his greatest triumphs in Amsterdam. He moved there in 1631 because, according to his first biographer Johannes Orlers, he was in great demand in the city. He lodged with the art dealer Hendrick van Uylenburgh in the St Anthoniebreestraat. With the great success, in 1632, of *The Anatomy Lesson* (*plate 10*), painted for Dr Nicolaes Tulp, a member of one of the city's leading families, he took Amsterdam by storm. From that year on his output of portraits is prodigious until it slackens in the last years of the decade. *Johannes Elison* and his wife, *Maria Bockenolle* (*plates 11 and 12*) are especially fine examples of the portraits of this period with their marked contrasts of light and shade and their firm draughtsmanship. Rembrandt's broader stroke and larger format replaced the previously fashionable stiff, detailed portraits of artists like Nicolaes Eliasz.

In 1634 Rembrandt married Hendrick van Uylenburgh's cousin, Saskia, the daughter of a wealthy family from Leeuwarden in Friesland. This was a time of great prosperity and, apparently, great personal happiness for Rembrandt. In 1639 he bought a house himself in the St Anthoniebreestraat. In order to buy the house he had to borrow heavily and he was never able to repay the loans. It was this burden, compounded by his financial irresponsibility in other transactions, that eventually brought about his bankruptcy and the sale of the house and his collection in 1657-8. The *Self-Portrait* (*plate 16*), now in the Norton Simon Museum at Pasadena, records, however, a happier time in the late 1630s when the fashionable world of Amsterdam applauded him. The slackening in the numbers of portrait commissions at the end of the 1630s has been thought to reflect a waning of his popularity, but it seems equally likely that, as a history painter, Rembrandt had become frustrated by the endless stream of time-consuming and unsatisfying portraits. Instead he turned increasingly to religious paintings and also to the medium of etching.

Huygens records that when he recommended Rembrandt to perfect his art by visiting Italy in order to study the masters of the Italian Renaissance, he replied that he was too busy and anyway many of the best Italian paintings were in Holland. Rembrandt's reply was without doubt facetious but it is now clear that he did see a considerable number of Italian paintings in Amsterdam. He also studied Italian art in the form of engravings. Leonardo, Raphael and Titian were his principal Italian influences, and a restraint, amounting almost to classicism, in his history paintings of the 1640s onwards can be traced to his study of the Italian High Renaissance.

In 1642 Saskia died, weakened by many pregnancies (their only child to survive, a son, Titus, had been born in 1641). This year of domestic tragedy saw the painting of a great work of Rembrandt's maturity, *The Night Watch* (*plate 19*). In this huge canvas the group portrait has become a history painting. The traditional format of the militiamen standing in rows or gathered around a dinner table has been transformed into a highly animated, unified composition. The myth which surrounds the picture is so persistent that it must be dispelled once again – there is no evidence to suggest that the militiamen were at all displeased with the picture (indeed, there is evidence to the contrary), nor are there any grounds to suppose that Rembrandt's financial problems of the 1650s had their beginning in the reception given to *The Night Watch*.

In the late 1640s and 1650s Rembrandt concentrated upon history painting and many of his greatest religious paintings, such as *Jacob Blessing the Sons of Joseph* (*plate 25*), date from these years. Confirmation of his continuing public success came with an important commission from Sicily in

1653 (*plate 24*), and in this connection we discover that the Italian painters Guercino and Mattia Preti were not only familiar with, but were enthusiastic about, the Dutch artist's work. (Two of Rembrandt's self-portraits hung in the Uffizi in Florence during the artist's lifetime.) Such examples are significant, for it needs to be stressed that Rembrandt was highly esteemed both inside and outside Holland during the 1650s and 1660s, which were decades of financial difficulties. In 1656, for example, the Amsterdam Surgeons' guild chose Rembrandt again to paint their group portrait (*The Anatomy Lesson of Dr Deyman* survives, though in a fragmentary state, in the Rijksmuseum, Amsterdam). As far as it is possible to follow the complex business of Rembrandt's finances, the declaration of bankruptcy in 1656 seems to have been brought about almost solely by his financial mismanagement. It reflects, too, on the low prices paid for works of art in Holland, where paintings were bought and sold in the manner of the modern art market, as opposed to, for example, Flanders, where the Church and the Court were the major patrons of art. Rubens, whose luxurious style of life Rembrandt may have had in mind when he bought his house and began to amass his collection, was paid far more for his paintings than Rembrandt ever received.

In 1660 Rembrandt's mistress, Hendrickje Stoffels, who had been with him since 1649 and had borne him a daughter in 1654, formed with Titus a company to employ the artist, which would then own all his paintings. This was a legal device to protect the artist's work from his creditors. Rembrandt and his household had moved to a new and quite spacious house in the Rozengracht, not at all the hovel of legend, where the artist had his studio. He continued to receive important commissions in Amsterdam: for example, the *Conspiracy of Julius Civilis* (*plates 32, 33*) for the new Town Hall in 1660, the group portrait of the *Staalmeesters* (*plate 39*) in 1662 and the *Equestrian Portrait of Frederik Rihel* (National Gallery, London) in 1663. When in 1661 Jacob and Margaretha (or Maria) Trip, patriarch and matriarch of the richest merchant dynasty in Holland, wished to have their portraits painted in order to present them to their sons, they chose Rembrandt; the miraculous portraits (*plates 34, 35*) hang today in the National Gallery in London. Such commissions confirm that while Rembrandt may not have been any longer at the very centre of the artistic life of Amsterdam (perhaps by his own wish, rather than by the vagaries of fashion), he was by no means forgotten.

A careful study of *Julius Civilis* will show how radically Rembrandt's style of history painting had changed from the highly finished, small-scale pictures of the Leiden years which had excited the interest of Huygens. In those early paintings, Rembrandt had created his effects by the precise depiction of each figure, all of whom registered their reactions to events by gesture or facial expression (horror, delight, and so on), as was required by contemporary artistic theory. This is obvious in *The Presentation in the Temple* (*plate 2*) of 1631, in which the response of each onlooker can be clearly seen. Soon after his arrival in Amsterdam, Rembrandt abandoned this almost miniaturistic technique for large-scale compositions in a dramatic, Caravaggesque style. This was not, however, his natural language and during the 1640s he evolved a new, quite personal approach to history painting. In this development *Christ and the Woman taken in Adultery* (*plate 15*) of 1644 is an important transitional painting. The encounter between Christ and the adulteress is broadly painted, with many of the surrounding figures suggested in the most schematic manner. Rembrandt had come to realize that concentration upon the key figures is far more effective in a scene of this kind than the careful depiction of the reactions of numerous bystanders. This concentration upon the essentials of a subject is central to the mature Rembrandt's approach to history painting. He reduces the number of figures in any one scene, and increases their scale in proportion to the total size of the canvas or panel. In *Jacob Blessing the Sons of Joseph* (*plate 25*) of 1656 all extraneous figures (with the possible exception of Asenath) have been removed in order to concentrate upon the central action. A decade later, in the great *Return of the Prodigal Son* (Leningrad), the process had gone even further with the two principal figures — the embracing father and son — given a monumentality which is the finest achievement in all Rembrandt's religious painting. *Julius Civilis* (*plates 32 and 33*) is similarly monumental, with its concentration upon the fateful oath which bound the Batavians in their resistance to the Roman invader.

As we should expect, Rembrandt's technique — the way in which he actually applied paint to canvas or panel — reflected these changes in his approach to the presentation of historical subjects. In the earliest pictures the paint is applied in a thin and sparing manner with details occasionally scraped into the wet paint with the end of the brush. Later the paint becomes increasingly thick, laid on with a loaded brush, as detail becomes less important. In the paintings of the last years, Rembrandt's lack of interest in detailed description had gone so far that he used a palette knife or even his fingers in broad strokes on the canvas. The increasing freedom of his brushwork in his late paintings is paralleled in his drawings and etchings.

The portraits too show a comparable progression, though obviously the need to present a likeness is a constant factor. The portraits that Rembrandt made soon after his arrival in Amsterdam, though often more broadly painted than those of other contemporary portraitists, are tighter, flatter and more precise in the application of paint than the heroic sequence of portraits from the 1650s — including *Jan Six* of 1654 (*plate 29*) and *Nicolaes Bruyningh* (*plate 28*) of 1655 — in which character is conveyed by Rembrandt not in the detailing of the features of the face but rather in pose and facial expression. For this reason the later portraits tend to adopt a half-length or full-length format, whereas the majority of the many portraits of the 1630s show heads alone.

Rembrandt's last years saw a succession of personal tragedies. Hendrickje, who had stood beside him during the difficult years of bankruptcy and the sale of his goods, died in 1663, and in 1668, his son Titus, who had married in the previous year, died. Yet if the self-portraits of these years show a troubled face, they also display a remarkable determination and strength of spirit. Rembrandt himself died in 1669, and was buried alongside Saskia and Titus in the Westerkerk.

1. *The Prophet Jeremiah Mourning over the Destruction of Jerusalem*

Signed and dated 1630. Panel. $22\frac{3}{4} \times 18in$ ($58 \times 46cm$)

The identification of the subject is not certain, but the burning city in the background is probably Jerusalem, which was put to the sword by Nebuchadnezzar, King of Babylon, as Jeremiah had prophesied: 'And (he) burned the house of the Lord, and the King's house; and all the houses of Jerusalem, and all the houses of the great men burned he with fire' (Jeremiah 52:13). The painting is dated 1630 and bears Rembrandt's Leiden monogram RHL (Rembrandt Harmensz. Leidensis). The model for the figure of the prophet may well have been Rembrandt's father, Harmen Gerritsz., whose appearance is recorded in a portrait drawing in Oxford. There are three other paintings of prophets, all on panel and all about the same size, from this period, which suggests that they formed a series commissioned by a single patron.

Amsterdam, Rijksmuseum

3. Self-Portrait

1629/30. Panel. $14\frac{3}{4} \times 11\frac{1}{2}$in (37·5 × 29cm)

This is the earliest of the five self-portraits included in this selection. Rembrandt's self-portraits, of which 60 or so survive, constitute a document of self-examination quite unique in the history of western painting until the series by Vincent van Gogh, who certainly had the example of his great Dutch predecessor in mind. In some respect the self-portraits were a response to a contemporary fashion — it was at this time that the Medici were assembling their great collection of artists' self-portraits at the Uffizi. However, no artist painted so many and at such regular intervals in his career. In this one Rembrandt has adopted a military persona, complete with a breastplate and long hair pulled into an untidy pigtail.

The Hague, Mauritshuis

4. *Christ in the Storm on the Sea of Galilee*

Signed and dated 1633. Canvas. 63 × 50in (160 × 127cm)

'And when he was entered into a ship, his disciples followed him. And, behold, there arose a great tempest in the sea, insomuch that the ship was covered with the waves: but he was asleep. And his disciples came to him, and awoke him, saying, Lord, save us: we perish. Then he saith unto them, Why are ye fearful, O ye of little faith? Then he arose, and rebuked the winds and the sea; and there was a great calm' (St Matthew 8:23–26). After he settled in Amsterdam, Rembrandt's many portrait commissions took up a large proportion of his time. He was able, however, to continue to paint religious scenes which he, in common with contemporary art theorists, considered to be a far more important category of painting than portraiture.

Rembrandt took the general scheme of this composition from an engraving after a painting by the late sixteenth-century Antwerp painter Marten de Vos.

Boston, Isabella Stewart Gardner Museum

5. *Portrait of Nicolaes Ruts*

Signed and dated 1631. Panel. 46 × 34⅜in (117 × 87·5cm)

This is one of the first Amsterdam portrait commissions that Rembrandt received, perhaps when he was still living in Leiden, for his move to Amsterdam took place in this year. Nicolaes Ruts (1573–1638) was a prosperous merchant in the city. It was with portraits such as these that Rembrandt quickly established himself as the most fashionable portrait painter in Amsterdam, painting in a much freer and more lively style than artists like Nicolaes Eliasz., whose pictures were stiff and more decorative by comparison.

New York, Frick Collection

6. *The Descent from the Cross*

c.1636. Panel. $34\frac{1}{4} \times 25\frac{3}{4}$in (89·4 × 65·2cm)

This is one of a series of pictures representing events of the Passion which Rembrandt painted for the Stadholder of Holland, Prince Frederik Henry of Orange. The commission came from the Prince's secretary, Constantijn Huygens, who had spotted Rembrandt's great promise in his Leiden years. We are unusually well informed about this commission as seven letters from Rembrandt to Huygens have survived, the only ones from Rembrandt's hand that we know. In the first letter, of 1636, Rembrandt writes that he is 'very diligently engaged in completing as quickly as possible the three Passion pictures, which His Excellency commissioned me to do: an Entombment, a Resurrection and an Ascension of Christ. These are companion pictures to Christ's Elevation and the Descent from the Cross.' From this letter it would seem that Rembrandt had already begun the first two, the Elevation and the Descent, on his own account before receiving the Stadholder's commission for the series. All five paintings are now in the Alte Pinakothek at Munich.

Munich, Alte Pinakothek

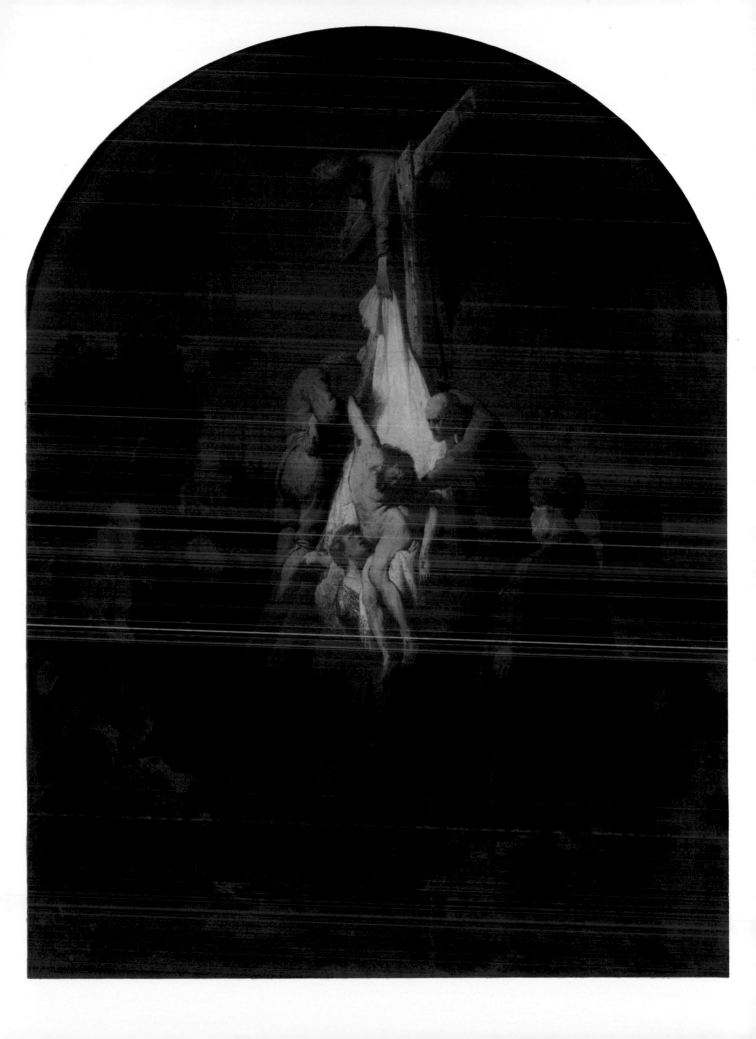

7. *The Blinding of Samson*

Signed and dated 1636. Canvas. 93 × 199in (236 × 302cm)

Rembrandt sent this painting as a gift to Constantijn Huygens, the secretary of the Prince of Orange, through whom he had received a commission for a series of paintings of the Passion (see *plate 6*). The letter which accompanied the painting survives. In a postscript Rembrandt wrote: 'The picture should be hung in a strong light and so that one can stand at a distance from it, then it will show its brilliance best.' The contemporary artist whom Huygens admired above all others was Rubens and the painting by Rubens which he praises at the greatest length in his autobiography is the gruesome *Head of Medusa*, now in Vienna. Rembrandt was no doubt aware of Huygens' taste for dramatic Baroque painting and had it in mind when painting this extravagantly violent account of Samson's blinding.

Frankfurt, Städelsches Kunstinstitut

8. *Self-Portrait with Saskia*

c.1634. Canvas. $63\frac{1}{4} \times 51\frac{1}{2}$in ($161 \times 131cm$)

Rembrandt painted this self-portrait with his wife Saskia on his knee soon after their marriage in June 1634. The setting is a tavern and X-rays of the picture show that originally Rembrandt had painted a lute-player in the picture on the left. The setting and the couple's rich clothes place the picture within the tradition of the representation of the story of the Prodigal Son who 'took his journey into a far country and there wasted his substance with riotous living' (St Luke 15:13). Why Rembrandt should represent himself as the Prodigal Son is unclear: perhaps it is a confession of the extravagant, wasteful side of his own character.

Dresden, Gemäldegalerie

9. *Saskia*

c.1635. Panel. $39\frac{1}{4} \times 31in$ (99·5 × 78·8cm)

With her face shown in strict profile, this is the most restrained and Italianate of Rembrandt's many portraits of his wife. It was probably painted in 1635, a year or so after their marriage. The richness of her dress, her pearls and fur display not only her own wealth (she was the daughter of a prosperous Leeuwarden family) but the rich style of life enjoyed by the young couple as a consequence of Rembrandt's great success as a portrait painter. Rembrandt sold this portrait to his friend Jan Six (*plate 30*) in 1652, ten years after Saskia's death.

Cassel, Gemäldegalerie

10. *The Anatomy Lesson of Dr Tulp*

Signed and dated 1632. Canvas. $66\frac{3}{4} \times 85\frac{1}{4}in$
(169·5 × 216·5cm)

Dr Nicolaes Pietersz. Tulp (1593–1674) was a leading Amsterdam surgeon, hailed by his contemporaries as the 'Amsterdam Vesalius'. (Vesalius was a Fleming who had revolutionized Renaissance anatomical studies in Padua in the sixteenth century.) The Anatomy Theatre in Amsterdam had been built at Tulp's request, and here he is seen demonstrating his anatomical skill in dissecting the muscles of the left arm. This is not a public dissection, for those always began with the abdominal cavity, but a private occasion. Tulp has dissected the brachial musculature and is demonstrating the mechanism of the hand with his own left hand. Only two members of his audience, whose names were added at a later date to the paper held by the man just to the left of Tulp, were members of the physicians' guild. It seems most likely that the painting does not record an actual event but was commissioned to honour the great anatomist. Rembrandt did not paint the dissected arm and hand from life but from an anatomical illustration in Adriaen van den Spiegel's *Humani Corporis Fabrica*. This may well be the volume open at the foot of the corpse. The *Anatomy Lesson* was Rembrandt's first major commission in Amsterdam, and played an important part in establishing his reputation there.

The Hague, Mauritshuis

11. *Johannes Elison*

Signed and dated 1634. Canvas. $68\frac{1}{8} \times 48\frac{7}{8}$in (173 × 124cm)

Johannes Elison was born in England in 1581. Like many
Puritan ministers he studied in Holland, enrolling at the
university of Leiden in 1598. From 1604 until his death
in 1639 he was a preacher at Norwich. One of his sons,
Johannes the Younger, moved to Amsterdam and there
became a successful businessman; his parents visited
him in 1634 and it was during this visit that they sat to
Rembrandt. The artist's evident sympathy with the
devout couple produced two of the finest of his early
Amsterdam portraits (this and *plate 12*). In the will made
by his son, the portraits were left to his brother-in-law
who lived in Norwich, where they remained — in the
same family — until the middle of the nineteenth century.

Boston, Museum of Fine Arts

12. *Maria Bockenolle, Wife of Johannes Elison*

Signed and dated 1634. Canvas. $68\frac{3}{4} \times 48\frac{7}{8}$ in (174·5 × 124cm)

See *plate 11*.

Boston, Museum of Fine Arts

13. *Susannah and the Elders*

Signed and dated 163(7?). Panel. $18\frac{3}{4} \times 15\frac{1}{4}$in
(47·5 × 39cm)

This Old Testament subject has traditionally given artists
a welcome opportunity to paint the female nude.
Rembrandt has exploited the chance to the full, no
doubt posing a model as Susannah. It was one of the
complaints made against Rembrandt's work by classicist
critics at the end of the century that he offended
decorum by giving his nudes heavy breasts, fat thighs
and even garter marks, rather than idealizing them. His
model here is painted naturalistically, a frightened
young girl whose natural modesty is offended by the two
elders who leer at her from their vantage point amid
the bushes.

The Hague, Mauritshuis

15. *Christ and the Woman Taken in Adultery*

Signed and dated 1644. Panel. $33 \times 25\frac{3}{4}$in ($83 \cdot 8 \times 65 \cdot 4$cm)

This account of Christ's forgiveness of the adulteress (St John 8:3) is an outstanding example of Rembrandt's small-scale religious scenes. It reveals his great gifts as a colourist, an aspect of his art which is often forgotten. In some ways it is an unexpected painting for the mid-1640s, for in the composition – the small figures dwarfed by the cavernous interior of the temple – as well as in the elaboration of detail and the degree of finish, particularly in the background, it harks back to paintings of the early 1630s such as *The Presentation of Jesus in the Temple (plate 2)*. The painting seems to be a deliberate return to an earlier phase in Rembrandt's career, but the broader treatment of the foreground group is consistent with other religious paintings of the 1640s.

London, National Gallery

16. *Self-Portrait*

c.1638/9. Panel. 24$\frac{1}{2}$ × 19$\frac{3}{4}$in (62·5 × 50cm)

This was painted probably around 1638/9 when Rembrandt was still enjoying enormous success as a portrait painter in Amsterdam. His prosperity is evident from his rich clothes and gold chain. His pose reflects his interest in Italian portraits (notably those by Raphael and Titian) which he saw when they passed through the busy international art market of Amsterdam.

Pasadena, California, Norton Simon Museum

17. *Agatha Bas, Wife of Nicolaes van Bambeeck*

Signed and dated 1641. Canvas. $41\frac{1}{2} \times 33in$ (105·5 × 84cm)

The couple depicted in this remarkable pair of portraits (Nicolaes van Bambeeck's is in the Musée Royal des Beaux-Arts in Brussels) is a good example of the lack of rigidity in Dutch society in the early years of the young Republic, which no doubt contributed to its great economic success. Agatha Bas, who was 29 when this portrait was painted, was a daughter of one of the oldest and most powerful families in the city. Nicolaes van Bambeeck was a new immigrant from Flanders who had settled in the city and rose from poverty to make a fortune as a merchant dealing in textiles. The couple lived in the St Anthoniebreestraat where Rembrandt and Saskia had bought a house in 1639. The personal ties are even closer, for in 1640 Bambeeck had lent money (as had Rembrandt) to the art dealer Hendrick van Uylenburgh, Saskia's cousin and Rembrandt's host when he first arrived in Amsterdam.

London, Buckingham Palace, Royal Collection (reproduced by gracious permission of Her Majesty the Queen)

19. *The Militia Company of Captain Frans Banning Cocq ('The Night Watch')*

Signed and dated 1642. Canvas. 143 × 172in (359 × 438cm)

The popular title of this, the best known of all Rembrandt's paintings, dates from the nineteenth century when the varnish on the picture had darkened considerably and the scene consequently appeared to be taking place at night. Recent cleaning has revealed that it is quite clearly set in the daytime. The commission probably came from Captain Frans Banning Cocq, the central figure. In his family album, now displayed near the painting in the Rijksmuseum, a seventeenth-century drawn copy of the picture is described as 'a sketch of the picture in the Great Room of the Civic Guards' House [Kloeveniersdoelen], in which the young lord of Purmerlandt [Banning Cocq] as captain gives orders to the lieutenant [Willem van Ruytenburgh, in yellow] to have his company march out'. The militia companies, or civic guards, had by 1642 acquired a social rather than a military function. Many group portraits of these companies survive (notably of the Haarlem companies by Frans Hals) but Rembrandt's treatment of them 'marching out' was novel as they were usually portrayed standing stiffly in rows or seated around a table. It is this dynamic composition which makes '*The Night Watch*' so effective. Early copies of the picture show that it was cut down on all sides (most severely on the left and at the top) when it was moved to the smaller War Council Chamber in the Town Hall in Amsterdam in 1715.

Amsterdam, Rijksmuseum

20. *'The Night Watch'*

Detail

Captain Frans Banning Cocq (centre) is seen giving orders to his lieutenant Willem van Ruytenburgh 'to have his company march out'. Behind the two officers is the cornet Jan Cornelisz. Visscher with the Amsterdam colours and two sergeants to the left and right (Reinier Engelen and Rombout Kemp). Although the commission probably came from Banning Cocq, sixteen of the Civic Guard officers and other ranks paid around 100 guilders each towards the cost of the painting 'the one more, the other less, according to their placing in the picture'. There is no evidence whatsoever to support the old legend that *'The Night Watch'* marked a turning point, for the worse, in Rembrandt's fortunes. The members of the company seem to have been perfectly satisfied with the picture and hung it in the Kloeveniersdoelen alongside the other militia group portraits.

Samuel van Hoogstraten, who was a pupil of Rembrandt when the picture was being painted, gave the best contemporary account of it. He stated that painters should not place their sitters in rows, as former painters of group portraits had done. The best masters created a unified composition. 'Rembrandt did this excellently in his militia piece in Amsterdam . . . this work, no matter how much it can be criticized [Hoogstraten was writing in the French-orientated classicizing climate of 1678] will survive its competitors because it is so painter-like in thought, so dashing in movement, and so powerful that according to some all the other pieces there [in the Kloeveniersdoelen] stand beside it like playing cards.'

21. *Hendrickje Stoffels (?) in Bed*

Late 1640s. Canvas. $32 \times 26\frac{1}{2}$in (81×67cm)

Only the first three digits of the date — 164 — are legible.
On stylistic grounds the painting must date from the
last years of the decade. Although the woman does have
a portrait quality, the real subject of the painting is
Sarah awaiting Tobias on her wedding night. Rembrandt
took the figure of Sarah from a painting of this subject
by his teacher, Pieter Lastman (now in the Boston
Museum of Fine Arts). The story, from the Apocrypha,
tells how Sarah had been married seven times before her
wedding to Tobias, but each time her husband had been
killed by the devil Asmodeus on the wedding night,
before the marriage could be consummated. In Lastman's
painting Sarah watches from the bed as Tobias burns
ash of perfume and the innards of a fish, and the Angel
Raphael appears to drive away Asmodeus. The couple
spend the rest of the night in prayer and the curse which
had hung over Sarah is finally lifted.

The identity of Rembrandt's model is uncertain. It
could be either Geertje Dircx or Hendrickje Stoffels, both
of whom entered Rembrandt's household as nurse to
Titus (Saskia had died in 1642) and subsequently
became the artist's mistress. Hendrickje had displaced
Geertje by 1649.

Edinburgh, National Gallery of Scotland

22. Winter Landscape

Signed and dated 1646. Panel. $6\frac{3}{4} \times 9in$ (17 × 23cm)

Rembrandt painted this sparkling winter landscape quickly and fluently. As can be clearly seen from a close examination, the signature and date were added when the paint was still wet. Rembrandt painted few landscapes and most of them are in a monochrome palette of greens and browns which shows the influence of the landscapist Hercules Segers. In this unique picture Rembrandt has employed a more colourful palette and seems to be experimenting with the landscape style of another Haarlem painter, Esaias van de Velde.

Cassel, Gemäldegalerie

23. *Bathsheba*

Signed and dated 1654. Canvas. 56 × 56in (142 × 142cm)

While her maid dries her feet after her bath, Bathsheba
meditates on the tragic implications of her having
caught the eye of King David. The king's letter is in her
hand and she seems to know that the consequence of
the king's passion will be the death of her husband
Uzziah.

It is likely that the model for the heavy figure of
Bathsheba was Hendrickje Stoffels, who bore the painter
a daughter, Cornelia, in the year of the *Bathsheba*, 1654.
Although at present darkened by a heavy discoloured
varnish, the painting is among the greatest of all
Rembrandt's many religious paintings.

Paris, Louvre

24. Aristotle with the Bust of Homer

Signed and dated 1653. Canvas. $56\frac{1}{2} \times 53\frac{3}{4}$in
(143·5 × 136·5cm)

The subject of a Greek philosopher is an unusual one for Rembrandt, and it is therefore no surprise to discover that the picture was painted as a particular commission. Count Antonio Ruffo, a collector living in Messina, ordered a 'philosopher, half figure' from Rembrandt, and the painting was despatched to Sicily in 1654. Ruffo later approached Guercino and Mattia Preti to paint companion pieces to the *Aristotle* but although both declared themselves happy (and indeed honoured) to emulate the Dutch painter, Ruffo returned to Rembrandt for the paintings. An *Alexander* (which has been variously identified with paintings now in Glasgow and Lisbon) and a *Homer* (in The Hague, Mauritshuis, although in a fragmentary state) were sent to Ruffo in 1661 and 1662. This Italian commission is an important reminder that the reputation of Dutch artists was by no means confined to the Netherlands.

New York, Metropolitan Museum of Art

25. *Jacob Blessing the Sons of Joseph*

Signed and dated 1656. Canvas. $69 \times 82\frac{3}{4}$in
(175·5 × 210·5cm)

The moment which Rembrandt represented is described in Genesis, 49:17–19: 'And when Joseph saw that his father laid his right hand upon the head of Ephraim, it displeased him: and he held up his father's hand, to remove it from Ephraim's head unto Manasseh's head. And Joseph said unto his father, Not so, for this is the first born; put thy right hand upon his head. And his father refused, and said, I know it, my son, I know it: he also shall become a people, and he also shall be great: but truly his younger brother shall be greater than he, and his seed shall become a multitude of nations.'

In Rembrandt's painting Jacob's hand rests on the head of the larger fair-haired child, Ephraim, from whom, according to the contemporary belief, the Gentiles traced their ancestry. The elder boy, Manasseh, who is small and dark, is blessed with the left hand. The submissive gesture of Ephraim's crossed hands, Joseph's tender regard for his father, Manasseh's intense gaze towards his brother, are all painted in strong, broad strokes. The unusual presence of Asenath, Joseph's wife, also in an attitude of submission, strengthens and balances the composition.

Cassel, Gemäldegalerie

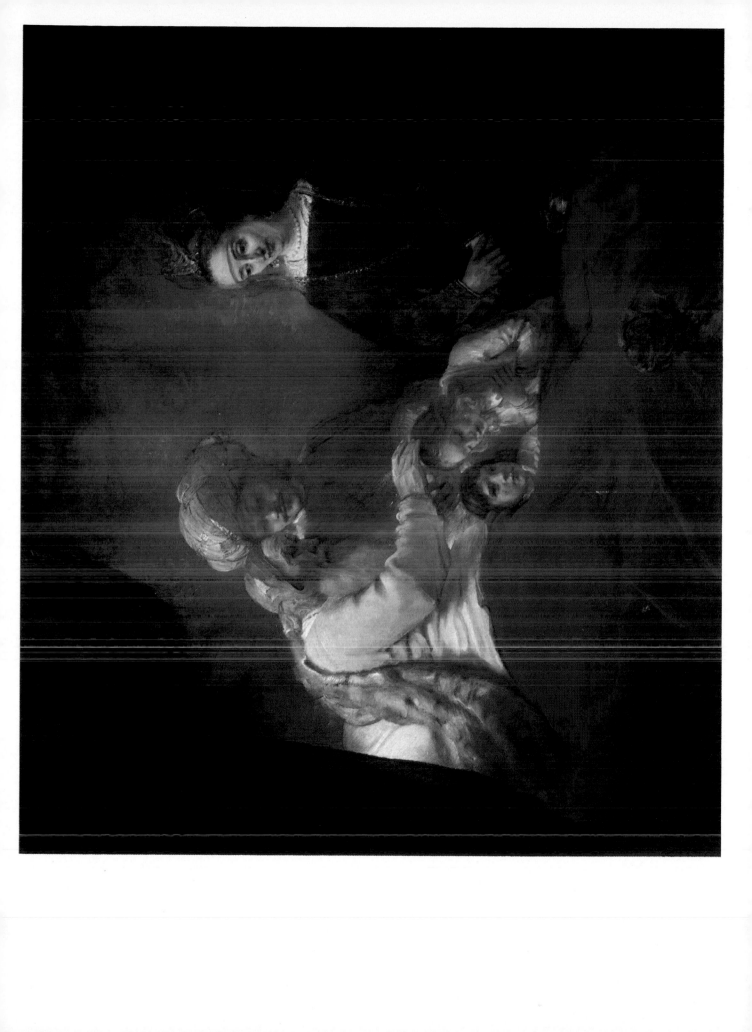

26. *The Polish Rider*

Mid-1650s. Canvas. 46 × 53⅛in (115 × 135·5cm)

Rembrandt only painted two equestrian portraits, this one in the mid-1650s and the *Portrait of Frederik Rihel* (National Gallery, London) in 1663. This painting is even more unusual among Rembrandt's portraits by virtue of the rider's dress and his weapons (a bow, a quiver of arrows and a war-hammer). There has been a great deal of discussion about the painting, which has been said to be an allegory of the Christian Knight in his fight against the infidel Turk. It has, however, been recently argued with great conviction that the painting is, more simply, a romanticized portrait of a young Polish nobleman, perhaps Szymon Karel Oginski, who like many of his compatriots studied at a Dutch university.

New York, Frick Collection

27. A Woman Bathing

Signed and dated 1654. Panel. $24\frac{5}{16} \times 18\frac{1}{2}$in ($62 \times 47$cm)

It has long been realized that the model for this painting was Rembrandt's mistress Hendrickje Stoffels. There is no certain portrait of Hendrickje, as there is of Saskia, but a group of portraits and studies from the years when she was living with the painter show the same sitter, and the tenderness with which they are painted makes it most likely that they show Hendrickje. The rich robe which has been left on the river bank makes it probable that this picture is a sketch for a never-executed mythological or religious painting. Hendrickje may be the model for Susannah or perhaps the goddess Diana.

The picture has the free handling appropriate to a sketch. The paint is firmly applied with broad strokes of a fully-loaded brush.

London, National Gallery

28. *Portrait of Nicolaes Bruyningh*

Signed and dated 1652. Canvas. $42\frac{1}{4} \times 36in$
(107·5 × 91·5cm)

Rembrandt's hectic output of portraits in the 1630s had greatly declined by the early 1650s. He preferred to concentrate on history paintings and on other media, especially etching. He did, however, continue to accept some commissions, and in the case of Bruyningh, the liveliness and enthusiasm of the sitter communicated themselves to the artist, and resulted in one of the finest of all his male portraits. Rembrandt was experimenting at this time with seated portraits, both painted and etched, and that of Bruyningh, with the sitter leaning, or so it seems, out of the chair towards the viewer, is the culmination of this group.

Cassel, Gemäldegalerie

29. *Portrait of Jan Six*

1654. Canvas. 44 × 40¼in (112 × 102cm)

We know the date of this portrait from a Latin poem written by Six about it: *AonIDas qVI sVM tenerIs VeneratVs ab annIs TaLIs ego IanVs SIXIVs ora tVLI* ('such a face had I, Jan Six, who since childhood have worshipped the Muses'). Read as Roman numerals and added up, the capital letters give the year 1654. Jan Six, who was born in 1618, was the son of a wealthy Amsterdam textile merchant. Educated at Leiden university, he travelled to Italy in 1640 and on his return became something of a *dilettante*. He wrote poetry, and formed a large collection of paintings, drawings and antique sculpture. Only in 1652, having taken little part in the family business, did he begin a career, as a city magistrate. It is in this serious and sober guise that he appears in this superb portrait, which has remained to this day in the collection of the Six family. Six was an important patron of Rembrandt, buying a number of paintings from him, and commissioning paintings and etchings. He also lent the artist a good deal of money and it was this that apparently soured relations between them in the late 1650s.

Amsterdam, Six Foundation

30. *Titus*

Signed and dated 1655. Canvas. 30 × 25in (77 × 63cm)

Titus, the only surviving child of Rembrandt's marriage
to Saskia, was born in 1641. There is no authenticated
portrait of him but there is a consensus that this picture,
the portrait of a *Young Man Reading* in Vienna, the
Young Man in a beret in the Wallace Collection (London)
and the pallid young man in a portrait in the Louvre all
show Titus at various stages of his short life. This is the
earliest of the portraits, and shows him as an eager
young student perched at his desk, his pen in one hand
and his inkwell in the other. He was not a robust boy
and the Louvre portrait shows the pale and sickly Titus
in about 1662 at the time of his marriage to Magdalena
van Loo. He died in the following year and his daughter
Titia was born posthumously.

Rotterdam, Museum Boymans-van Beuningen

31. *Self-Portrait*

c.1657/8. Panel. 19 × 16in (49 × 41cm)

This was painted at the height of Rembrandt's financial troubles. The face may be worried and the clothes more modest than in earlier self-portraits, but the artist's skill shows no failing whatsoever. Indeed, the second half of the 1650s saw a succession of magnificent religious paintings and of portraits.

Vienna, Kunsthistorisches Museum

32. *The Conspiracy of Julius Civilis*

c.1660–2. Canvas. 77 × 121in (196 × 309cm)

Jacob van Campen's great Town Hall on the Dam at Amsterdam was inaugurated in 1655. The city fathers decided soon afterwards to decorate the interior with a series of paintings representing the revolt of the Batavians against the Romans. The Batavian revolt was seen by contemporaries as a prototype of the struggle of the Dutch against the Spanish and Julius Civilis, the leader of that revolt, was identified with William the Silent. The commission for the series went to Govaert Flinck, who had been a pupil of Rembrandt in the 1640s. Flinck completed only the first scene, and had sketched out four more at the time of his death in February 1660. Rembrandt was the first artist to be commissioned in Flinck's place. He was to paint a nocturnal scene, the swearing of the oath to resist the Romans. The other commissions went to Jan Lievens and Jacob Jordaens. All the canvases were in place by July 1662.

Stockholm, Nationalmuseum

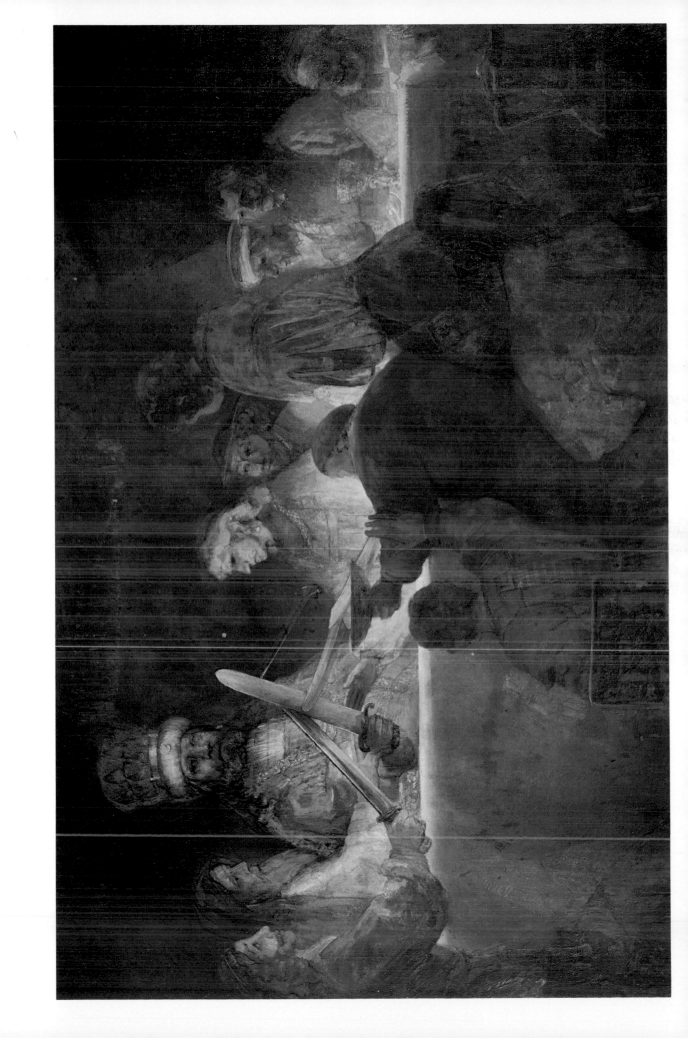

33. *The Conspiracy of Julius Civilis*
Detail

Although it was accepted and hung in the Town Hall,
Rembrandt's painting was taken down, probably in
1663, and replaced with a canvas by Jurriaen Ovens,
who seems simply to have completed Flinck's sketch.
Rembrandt's painting was subsequently cut down,
perhaps by the artist himself. The reason for the
rejection of the painting is not known, but it is possible
that his depiction of the national hero as a one-eyed
barbarian chieftain (in this he followed the classical
source, Tacitus) was not decorous enough for the city
fathers of Amsterdam.

35. *Maria Trip*

Early 1660s. Canvas. $51\frac{3}{8} \times 38\frac{3}{8}$in (130·5 ×97·5cm)

This portrait of Maria Trip is a companion to that of her husband (*plate 34*). Jacob and Maria Trip lived in Dordrecht and presumably sat for these portraits while visiting their sons in Amsterdam. The paintings were destined to be hung in their sons' residence, the *Trippenhuis*. The National Gallery in London also has a bust portrait of Maria which was painted at the same time, presumably in connection with this commission. In both, Maria wears a mill-stone ruff and a dress which had long been out of fashion.

London, National Gallery

37. 'The Jewish Bride'

c.1665/6. Canvas. 48 × 65½in (121·5 × 166·5cm)

The painting is signed and dated, but only the first three digits of the date can be read, 166. It was probably painted in 1665/6. The title is a traditional one and there is no certainty about the painting's real subject. There is a drawing (Private Collection, New York) representing the Biblical love story of Isaac and Rebecca (Genesis 26:8) which seems to have been the first idea for the picture. Whether the painting represents that Biblical story or is a double portrait in the guise of the story is unclear. What is certain, however, is that the picture is a poignant evocation of middle-aged love rendered in the strong colours and broad technique (the paint is applied with a palette knife as well as with a brush) of Rembrandt's last years.

Amsterdam, Rijksmuseum

39. 'The Staalmeesters' (The Sampling-Officials of the Clothmakers' Guild)

Signed and dated 1662. Canvas. 75 × 110in (191 × 279cm)

The painting formerly hung in the Staalhof, the clothmakers' office, in Amsterdam where four different committees held their meetings. The sitters for this group portrait were the *Waerdijns van der Laekenen*, the controllers of the cloth samples, who served for a one-year term, starting on Good Friday. These men are the officials who served for the year 1661/2. The steep viewpoint of the picture was chosen to accord with the position in which it was to hang. The man who starts up from his chair is a compositional device by Rembrandt to make the portrait more immediate. There is no question, as has been suggested, of his rising to address a public meeting. The book which two men hold, and which provides a focus for the composition, is a sample book of cloth which acted as a standard for judging other cloths, and it was the maintenance of this standard which the officials were appointed to ensure. The whole painting is a symbol of good citizenship and good government.

Amsterdam, Rijksmuseum

40. *St Matthew and the Angel*

Signed and dated 1661. Canvas. 38 × 32in (96 × 81cm)

Rembrandt painted a number of half-length single saints in the early 1660s. These have been considered to be a series but the unevenness of their quality and small variations in size make this unlikely. This is one of the finest and best preserved of this group. The model for St Matthew's attribute, the angel, was Rembrandt's son, Titus, who in 1661 was 20 years old.

Paris, Louvre

Acknowledgements, and list of illustrations and sources

THE AUTHOR AND BLACKER CALMANN COOPER LTD would like to thank the museums and owners who allowed works in their collections to be reproduced in this book. Unless otherwise stated they provided the transparencies used. The author and Blacker Calmann Cooper Ltd would also like to thank the photographers and photographic agencies who provided transparencies.

1. *The Prophet Jeremiah Mourning over the Destruction of Jerusalem* — Amsterdam, Rijksmuseum
2. *The Presentation of Jesus in the Temple* — The Hague, Mauritshuis
3. *Self-Portrait* — The Hague, Mauritshuis
4. *Christ in the Storm on the Sea of Galilee* — Boston, Isabella Stewart Gardner Museum
5. *Portrait of Nicolaes Ruts* — Copyright the Frick Collection, New York
6. *The Descent from the Cross* — Munich, Alte Pinakothek
7. *The Blinding of Samson* — Frankfurt, Städelsches Kunstinstitut. Photo Blauel
8. *Self-Portrait with Saskia* — Dresden, Gemäldegalerie
9. *Saskia* — Cassel, Gemäldegalerie
10. *The Anatomy Lesson of Dr Tulp* — The Hague, Mauritshuis
11. *Johannes Elison* — Boston, Museum of Fine Arts
12. *Maria Bockenolle, Wife of Johannes Elison* — Boston, Museum of Fine Arts
13. *Susannah and the Elders* — The Hague, Mauritshuis
14. *A Man Standing in Front of a Doorway* — Cassel, Gemäldegalerie
15. *Christ and the Woman Taken in Adultery* — London, National Gallery (by courtesy of the Trustees)
16. *Self-Portrait* — Pasadena, Norton Simon Museum
17. *Agatha Bas, Wife of Nicolaes van Bambeeck* — London, Buckingham Palace (by gracious permission of Her Majesty the Queen)
18. *Cornelis Claesz. Anslo in Conversation with a Woman* — Berlin-Dahlem, Gemäldegalerie. Photo Fournier
19. *The Militia Company of Captain Frans Banning Cocq ('The Night Watch')* — Amsterdam, Rijksmuseum
20. *Detail of plate 19*
21. *Hendrickje Stoffels (?) in Bed* — Edinburgh, National Gallery of Scotland
22. *Winter Landscape* — Cassel, Gemäldegalerie
23. *Bathsheba* — Paris, Louvre. Photo Musées Nationaux
24. *Aristotle with the Bust of Homer* — New York, Metropolitan Museum
25. *Jacob Blessing the Sons of Joseph* — Cassel, Gemäldegalerie
26. *The Polish Rider* — Copyright the Frick Collection, New York
27. *A Woman Bathing* — London, National Gallery
28. *Portrait of Nicolaes Bruyningh* — Cassel, Gemäldegalerie
29. *Portrait of Jan Six* — Amsterdam, Six Foundation
30. *Titus* — Rotterdam, Museum Boymans-van Beuningen
31. *Self-Portrait* — Vienna, Kunsthistorisches Museum
32. *The Conspiracy of Julius Civilis* — Stockholm, Nationalmuseum
33. *Detail of plate 32*
34. *Jacob Trip* — London, National Gallery
35. *Maria Trip* — London, National Gallery
36. *Family Group* — Brunswick, Herzog Anton-Ulrich Museum
37. *'The Jewish Bride'* — Amsterdam, Rijksmuseum
38. *Self-Portrait* — London, Kenwood House, Iveagh Bequest (GLC). Photo Cooper-Bridgeman Library
39. *'The Staalmeesters'* — Amsterdam, Rijksmuseum
40. *St Matthew and the Angel* — Paris, Louvre. Photo Musées Nationaux

Acknowledgements, and list of illustrations and sources

THE AUTHOR AND BLACKER CALMANN COOPER LTD would like to thank the museums and owners who allowed works in their collections to be reproduced in this book. Unless otherwise stated they provided the transparencies used. The author and Blacker Calmann Cooper Ltd would also like to thank the photographers and photographic agencies who provided transparencies.

1. *The Prophet Jeremiah Mourning over the Destruction of Jerusalem* — Amsterdam, Rijksmuseum
2. *The Presentation of Jesus in the Temple* — The Hague, Mauritshuis
3. *Self-Portrait* — The Hague, Mauritshuis
4. *Christ in the Storm on the Sea of Galilee* — Boston, Isabella Stewart Gardner Museum
5. *Portrait of Nicolaes Ruts* — Copyright the Frick Collection, New York
6. *The Descent from the Cross* — Munich, Alte Pinakothek
7. *The Blinding of Samson* — Frankfurt, Städelsches Kunstinstitut. Photo Blauel
8. *Self-Portrait with Saskia* — Dresden, Gemäldegalerie
9. *Saskia* — Cassel, Gemäldegalerie
10. *The Anatomy Lesson of Dr Tulp* — The Hague, Mauritshuis
11. *Johannes Elison* — Boston, Museum of Fine Arts
12. *Maria Bockenolle, Wife of Johannes Elison* — Boston, Museum of Fine Arts
13. *Susannah and the Elders* — The Hague, Mauritshuis
14. *A Man Standing in Front of a Doorway* — Cassel, Gemäldegalerie
15. *Christ and the Woman Taken in Adultery* — London, National Gallery (by courtesy of the Trustees)
16. *Self-Portrait* — Pasadena, Norton Simon Museum
17. *Agatha Bas, Wife of Nicolaes van Bambeeck* — London, Buckingham Palace (by gracious permission of Her Majesty the Queen)
18. *Cornelis Claesz. Anslo in Conversation with a Woman* — Berlin-Dahlem, Gemäldegalerie. Photo Fournier
19. *The Militia Company of Captain Frans Banning Cocq ('The Night Watch')* — Amsterdam, Rijksmuseum
20. *Detail of plate 19*
21. *Hendrickje Stoffels (?) in Bed* — Edinburgh, National Gallery of Scotland
22. *Winter Landscape* — Cassel, Gemäldegalerie
23. *Bathsheba* — Paris, Louvre. Photo Musées Nationaux
24. *Aristotle with the Bust of Homer* — New York, Metropolitan Museum
25. *Jacob Blessing the Sons of Joseph* — Cassel, Gemäldegalerie
26. *The Polish Rider* — Copyright the Frick Collection, New York
27. *A Woman Bathing* — London, National Gallery
28. *Portrait of Nicolaes Bruyningh* — Cassel, Gemäldegalerie
29. *Portrait of Jan Six* — Amsterdam, Six Foundation
30. *Titus* — Rotterdam, Museum Boymans-van Beuningen
31. *Self-Portrait* — Vienna, Kunsthistorisches Museum
32. *The Conspiracy of Julius Civilis* — Stockholm, Nationalmuseum
33. *Detail of plate 32*
34. *Jacob Trip* — London, National Gallery
35. *Maria Trip* — London, National Gallery
36. *Family Group* — Brunswick, Herzog Anton-Ulrich Museum
37. *'The Jewish Bride'* — Amsterdam, Rijksmuseum
38. *Self-Portrait* — London, Kenwood House, Iveagh Bequest (GLC). Photo Cooper-Bridgeman Library
39. *'The Staalmeesters'* — Amsterdam, Rijksmuseum
40. *St Matthew and the Angel* — Paris, Louvre. Photo Musées Nationaux